THOMAS AQUINAS IN 90 MINUTES

Thomas Aquinas
IN 90 MINUTES

Paul Strathern

IVAN R. DEE
CHICAGO

Library of Congress Cataloging-in-Publication Data:
Strathern, Paul, 1940–
    Thomas Aquinas in 90 minutes / Paul Strathern.
      p.   cm. — (Philosophers in 90 minutes)
    Includes bibliographical references and index.
    ISBN 1-56663-193-9 (cloth : alk. paper). —
ISBN 1-56663-194-7 (pbk. : alk. paper)
    1. Thomas, Aquinas, Saint, 1225?–1274.   I. Title.
II. Series.
B765.T54S764   1998
189'.4—dc21   98-13264

Contents

CONTENTS

THOMAS AQUINAS IN 90 MINUTES

Introduction

Thomas Aquinas died on March 7, 1274, and ascended to heaven. Forty-nine years later he became a saint; and in 1879 Pope Leo XIII pronounced that Aquinas's work was "the only true philosophy."

Aquinas thus made a break with the great philosophical tradition of getting things wrong. This sets him apart from all other philosophers (and perhaps even from philosophy itself). Indeed, there would seem to be nothing more to say on the matter. Unless, that is, you happen to believe that our thinking has made some advances since the era of the Children's Crusade and the chastity belt.

Being the subject of many a sickly hagiography, filled with winsome anecdotes and unquestioning acceptance of much metaphysical twaddle, has done little for Aquinas's philosophical reputation. All we see is a shadowy figure amongst the incense clouds of theology. It is difficult to discern the finest philosophical mind in Europe for a thousand years (since St. Augustine). Yet Aquinas is unquestionably of this stature.

In order to appreciate Aquinas it is necessary to distinguish, as far as possible, between his theology and his philosophy. The former is absolutely correct on all counts, and beyond question. (Anyone who doubts this courts instant excommunication and the prospect of an afterlife in a third-world-style region devoid of modern domestic conveniences.) Philosophy, on the other hand, is something whose truth is open to question. This is what makes philosophy what it *is*.

Even in Aquinas's time there was an implicit difference between theology and philosophy. Both conducted their arguments in a similar fashion—by deduction, reason, logic, and so forth. But in theology such knowledge was based upon the revealed truth of faith. The first principles of theology were supported by a belief in God. Philosophy, on the other hand, required no such belief. It began from first principles which were allegedly "self-evident." These relied upon our apprehension of the world around us and the use of reason alone.

In practice, of course, theology and philosophy often overlapped—especially in the religion-dominated civilization of the medieval era. Such a state of affairs may appear quaint in these godless times, but in fact our thinking is reduced to an uncannily similar state. Modern philosophy merely papers over the divide between theological and philosophical thinking. Even to philosophize, we must start with a belief in something—basic assumptions, which remain beyond our ability to prove by reason. For example, a belief in the coherence and consistency of the world, without which there could be no scientific laws. But surely this is just quibbling? Isn't this what "self-evident" means? It's *obvious* the world is coherent, even if we have no way of proving it. Not so. Modern quantum mechanics, which deals with the behavior of subatomic particles, has neither coherence nor causality. This is of course science, and it is possible that we will soon come up with some overall theory (a theory of everything, say) which will overcome such apparent inconsistencies. But this is not the point. Under present conditions a belief in the ultimate consistency of the world is no more justifiable than a belief in God. In fact, this remains true *under any conditions.*

Which brings us to another relevant comparison. The late twentieth century is almost unimaginably different from the medieval era. The contemporary mind in an advanced technological society bears precious little resemblance to a medieval mind. Some philosophers and scientists have even begun to question whether these two individuals share such a thing as a common humanity. They argue that there is no such thing, only an ever-evolving species. For them, the concept of "humanity" implies such outmoded entities as a "soul," an unvarying "human condition," a "conscious-ness" which eludes scientific pinpointing, a belief in the uniqueness of "individuality" and such—notions which have no place in a world of Darwinian evolution, DNA, cloning, and similar miracles which have contributed to modern self-understanding.

In which case, what possible relevance has Thomas Aquinas to us? The simple souls who cannot accept such an extremist scientific view—obstinately clinging to the notion that Hamlet, Faust, and even Dante still have something to say to us—will need little convincing. Those who believe that we are in the initial throes of an un-precedented era of human development (amounting to a fundamental evolutionary transformation) will need more persuading. But a case can be made. Progress in the six hundred years between Aquinas and the start of the twen-tieth century was to all intents a leisurely amble. By the end of the twentieth century this has quickened to a headlong dash. If we consider that the worldview (or mind-set) of Aquinas has become an irrelevancy over the centuries, how much shorter before ours too joins the scrap heap? If progress is a film sequence, must every present frame be regarded as the only picture we see? "Serious" modern thinkers may regard Aquinas much as we regard early Chaplin. How long before our thought processes are regarded like knockabout farce? Or might the cliché banana skins and saccharine sentimentality of Chaplin still have something to say to us?

We see our age as the greatest in human history (a delusion shared by many previous ages). Ours is a time of seemingly unending originality, yet such protean dynamism is not a necessary characteristic of great eras. Amongst the most long-lasting and stable civilizations, upon which vast intellectual and material resources were lavished, were those in China and medieval Europe. Here stasis was achieved, and with it a stability that enabled the development of structured thought and intellectual embellishment to an unparalleled degree. Dante's *Divine Comedy* was perhaps the finest poetic construction humanity has yet produced, and the certainties it embodied were part and parcel of the medieval age. The vast gothic cathedrals of western Europe were arguably the first great *collective* monuments of humanity. They incorporated the disparate talents of their builders; and not since ancient Greece had works of such magnificence been produced without the goad of tyranny. The medieval age also produced its own collective monument of the intellect. Truly a mammoth of thought, this was the largely static, cumulative philosophy of Scholasticism. And the acknowledged maestro of Scholastic philosophy was Thomas Aquinas.

Aquinas's Life and Works

Thomas Aquinas (Tommaso d'Aquino) was born in a castle four miles north of Aquino, in southern Italy. This rather gloomy castle still stands on the hill above the village of Roccasecca, just off the autostrada between Rome and Naples. Thomas was the seventh son of Count Landolfo d'Aquino; and the celebrated lyric poet Rinaldo d'Aquino may well have been one of his brothers. More interestingly, Thomas was the nephew of Frederick II, the maverick Holy Roman Emperor whose court in Sicily was the scene of a premature Renaissance. A man of exceptional talents, Frederick was excommunicated by the pope, but then set off on his own crusade which retook Jerusalem for Christendom (thus placing the pope in something of a quandary).

When Thomas was five he was sent to school with the monks at Monte Cassino. Here his acute intellect and religious temperament soon became apparent. But after nine years his education was interrupted when Uncle Frederick expelled the monks, because he reckoned they were becoming too friendly with his enemy the pope. Thomas was then sent to the University of Naples, which had been founded by Frederick. (Unfortunately by this time Frederick had also decided to found a new religion, with himself as messiah; and when his chief minister turned down the job of St. Peter, he had him blinded and displayed in a cage.)

Under the protection of Frederick II the University of Naples had become an important center for the new knowledge that was beginning to spread through the medieval world. Classical learning was being rediscovered, and the University of Naples attracted learned men from the farthest corners of Europe. Thomas was taught logic by a learned Transylvanian called Master

16

Martin, and he attended lectures on natural philosophy (science) given by Master Peter of Hibernia (Ireland).

It was Master Martin who introduced Thomas Aquinas to Aristotle's treatises on logic, which played such a dominant role in medieval thinking. Aristotle is generally credited with the invention of logic in the fourth century B.C. The word *logic* derives from the Greek *logos* (word, or language) and originally meant something akin to "the rules of discourse." Aristotle regarded logic as an *organon* (tool) for use in philosophy. As such, it could be used in every branch of knowledge. The purpose of logic was *analytika*, "to unravel."

But the logic that Aquinas inherited in the thirteenth century had made very little advance in the millennia since it had been invented by Aristotle. Its main form of argument was the syllogism, described by Aristotle as "an argument where certain facts are set down, and these facts generate further knowledge which necessarily follows." A simple example of a syllogism is as follows:

All human beings are mortal.
All Greeks are human beings.
Therefore all Greeks are mortal.

When it was used by Aristotle, this tripartite mode of argument proved highly productive, liberating thought and leading to new knowledge. The basic structure of Aristotle's logic remained sound in Aquinas's time, but its methods were beginning to become stale and restrictive. Argument was viewed as little more than a ritual employment of logical method, rather than the tool that Aristotle had intended. Such methods were regarded as the holy writ, and little attempt was made to improve upon them. Aquinas's quick brain soon enabled him to become adept at this verbal dexterity. He also found himself drawn to more profound philosophical speculations and realized that such methods could be used here too, in order to clarify his thoughts.

At the same time Aquinas found himself increasingly attracted by the Dominicans. This monastic order had been founded just over a quarter-century earlier in 1215 by St. Dominic, a Castillian of fanatical orthodoxy. The purpose of

18

the order was to stamp out heresy. Its members wore black robes and had originally wandered the countryside relying on alms for their subsistence. But recently the order had become more oriented toward learning, which under St. Dominic had been forbidden—like soft mattresses—without special dispensation.

Thomas Aquinas's decision to join the Dominicans caused consternation in his family. Mindful of his exceptional intellect and religious temperament, they had encouraged him to join the church. With his talents and family connections he could easily have become archbishop of Naples, a suitably prestigious position for a descendant of the military commander of the Holy Roman Empire (Thomas's grandfather, after whom he was named). But the thought of an Aquino wandering the highways of Italy, penniless and begging, met with a reaction similar to a modern general's son hitching off to join a hippy colony in the caves of Crete.

Yet Thomas was determined. He saw himself as following in the footsteps of another scion of a prestigious family who had recently given up everything for his beliefs—Francis of Assisi. Some two decades earlier Francis had founded the order named after him. He had dedicated his life to caring for the sick and the destitute, a term he stretched to include the animals and the birds, whom he regarded as his brothers. Thomas was to remain inspired by the example of St. Francis throughout his life, despite their deep differences in aim and temperament. When Thomas was found muttering on his own, he would be working his way through an Aristotelian proof rather than having a fraternal chat with the birds.

Before Thomas's parents could act to stop him, he joined the Dominicans and gave up his studies at Naples. The freshly fledged young Dominican now set off to walk to Paris, his mind filled with new ideas from the works of Aristotle, exhilarated by the prospect of a life of holy penury devoted to study. Paris was the greatest center of learning in Christendom. Thomas wished to study there with Albertus Magnus, one of the finest scholars of the age, who was renowned for his commentaries on Aristotle.

The nineteen-year-old Thomas managed to get eighty miles down the road, as far as the shores of Lake Bolsano, north of Rome. Then his brothers, who had been dispatched on horseback by his mother, caught up with him. Immediately they set upon Thomas, bound him, and carried him back to the family castle at Roccasecca. Here Thomas was imprisoned in a tower. In order to bring him to his senses, his father offered to fix him up with the post of abbot of Monte Cassino (now refurbished by Frederick II with monks who regarded the pope less favorably). But Thomas wasn't interested in returning to become headmaster of his old school. What were the Aquinases to do with their obstinate offspring, who appeared determined to become a socially inferior saint? Thomas's mother, who was of down-to-earth Norman stock, decided to try a more French approach—and introduced a buxom young peasant girl into Thomas's tower one cold winter's night.

According to the story, Thomas was attempting to coax a fire into life on the floor of his cell when the girl entered. He looked up, and

21

through the flames he saw this apparition. He knew at once that his eyes were deceiving him. This wasn't a scantily dressed young girl offering herself for a night of wild abandoned love—this was a salamander: a spirit of lust conjured up by some devilish magic. Thomas snatched a flaming faggot from the fire and brandished it at the girl. At once the apparition disappeared, fleeing through the door in case her inflammatory garb proved more inflammatory than she'd bargained for. In a state of ecstasy at his miraculous deliverance from this wanton spirit, Thomas raised the flaming faggot and drew a sign on his cell wall. According to tradition, this was the sign of the cross.

Thomas was to remain locked up in the family tower for a year, during which he read the Bible and studied Aristotle's *Metaphysics*. This was the title given to a dozen or so of Aristotle's short treatises which discuss, among other topics, the question of being (ontology) and the ultimate nature of things. The word *metaphysics*, which has become almost synonymous with philosophy, derives from the ancient Greek, meaning "above (or beyond) physics." In this work Aristotle attempts to discover what conditions are true of all existent beings. Famously he asks: "What is substance?" and goes on to discuss the difference between substance and essence, or matter and form. Aristotle rejected the Platonic notion that matter received its particular shape and identity from an ideal world of abstract forms. For Aristotle the form of a particular object is in many ways as concrete as its matter or substance. The form is regarded as its essence.

In the latter part of his *Metaphysics,* Aristotle discusses theology. He asks what is the cause of something, then asks what causes this cause, and so on. In this way he traces back along the causal chain to the ultimate cause of things, the prime mover, which is itself unmoving. This he identifies as God. Such arguments were readily acceptable to the Christian church. Aristotle's proof of God's existence gave philosophical backing (and thus intellectual respectability) to Christian faith. These remnants of Aristotle's thought, along with similar remnants of Plato, had thus survived the Europe of the Dark Ages. They had been absorbed into the canon of Christian teaching, which had remained preserved in remote religious communities, before emerging to become the dominant intellectual force in medieval Europe. Although the ideas put forward by Plato and Aristotle couldn't possibly have been Christian (they had both died more than three hundred years before the birth of Christ), this was not considered relevant. Yet, as we shall see, this left such things as Aristotle's proof of the existence of God in a somewhat anomalous position (that is, precisely which God's existence had he proved?).

The young Aquinas, avidly devouring Aristotle's *Metaphysics* in his prison tower, also chose to overlook any possible differences between Aristotle's God and the Christian God he believed in so fervently. What impressed him was Aristotle's peerless intellect, his questioning of the ultimate nature of things, and his ability to prove God's existence. Such philosophical argument was meat and drink to his awakening intellect.

But all good things must come to an end.

Aquinas was not to remain undisturbed in his tower indefinitely. Eventually his sister hatched a plan for his escape. In this she was assisted by some of his brothers, who had now become more sympathetic. (One hopes that Rinaldo the poet was among them, but there is no evidence.) Late at night Thomas's sister and his brothers crept into the tower and lowered Thomas in a basket over the walls. By next morning he was back on the road to Paris—making sure he kept a low profile amongst the traveling pilgrims, knights, wives from Bath, simpletons, and piemen on their way to the fair.

After tramping up through Lombardy, over the Alps, and across Burgundy, covering almost a thousand miles on foot, Thomas arrived in Paris. Here he discovered that Albertus Magnus had gone to teach at Cologne in Germany. Three hundred miles later, Thomas arrived at Cologne.

Albertus Magnus was a Swabian, whose teaching was instrumental in the revival of student interest in Aristotle. (He was belatedly canonized, for no apparent reason, in 1931. Now known as St. Albert the Great, he is the patron saint of natural scientists who feel the need of protection from heretical beliefs—a category into which almost every major scientific advance has fallen at some stage.) Albertus Magnus was quickly impressed by the gauche twenty-three-year-old from southern Italy. Thomas Aquinas had grown into a rather awkward giant. He could express even the most complex ideas with utmost clarity, yet he was all but incapable of expressing his feelings (except with the aid of a flaming faggot). His large oxlike eyes would stare out imploringly as his rowdy fellow students ragged him unmercifully—though from a safe distance. He soon became known as "the dumb ox," though Albertus Magnus is said to have reproved Aquinas's tormentors: "Mark my words, one day the lowing of that ox will be heard all over Christendom." This story, typical of the flimsy hagiographic anecdote that attaches itself to someone about whom there's not much else to say, nonetheless seems to confirm a rather bovine manner and appearance.

Eventually Albertus Magnus returned to Paris, and Thomas accompanied him. Besides being the finest center of learning in Europe, the University of Paris had a unique freedom in the medieval world. Its students and teachers were nominally clerics, and were thus not answerable to the civil authorities. Yet owing to a jealously guarded statute, they were also free from the clerical jurisdiction of the bishop of Paris and answerable only directly to Rome. In an age when the mail took over a fortnight to reach Rome (as it does once again today), this left the university and its students with a fair amount of leeway. In the next century this anomaly was to allow the poet François Villon, who committed a murder while a student in Paris, to escape the gallows. But in Aquinas's time the main trouble was not so much rowdyism as new ideas. Then, as now, Paris's Latin Quarter was a ferment of the latest ideas which no one else could even begin to understand, let alone believe in. The poststructuralism of the thirteenth century was the reemergence of classical learning, especially further works of Aristotle which had not previously been known.

Classical learning had become fragmented

after the collapse of the Roman Empire. The teachings of such as Plato and Aristotle had survived only in limited form. Many ancient manuscripts had been scattered, destroyed, or lost. In the fifth century Aristotle is known to have been translated by Nestorian Christians into Syraic (an ancient variant of Aramaic, spoken in Syria). During the ensuing centuries his works were translated into Hebrew and Arabic. Then in the twelfth century the great Islamic scholar Averroës came across Aristotle's work. Averroës (who might not have achieved such renown if he had insisted upon being known by his proper Arabic name Abu al Walid Muhammed ibn Ahmad ibn Muhammed ibn Rushd) was a judge in Moorish-occupied Spain, at the city of Qurtubah (Cordoba). In the manner of the Islamic scholars of his age, Averroës was also a physician and a philosopher. When he became personal physician to the calif of Cordoba, his master persuaded him to write a series of commentaries on Aristotle. These were then translated into Latin, the international language spoken throughout intellectual Europe, which united the continent's culture in a manner that eludes us today.

When Averroës's commentaries began appearing in Europe they reawakened interest in Aristotle, whose scientific spirit was particularly attuned to the changes taking place in the medieval world. Feudalism was on the wane, and Europe was witnessing the growth of cities whose urbanized populations were developing a new attitude toward the world.

Christianity had already had one encounter with Greek thought eight hundred years earlier. On that occasion it had absorbed various Platonic ideas, assisted by St. Augustine. But these ideas had merely confirmed Christianity in its contempt for everyday reality. The world was but the poor stage upon which humanity underwent the drama of its spiritual struggles. True reality lay in the transcendent realm of pure ideas: all else was at best a distraction, at worst an enslavement leading to eternal damnation.

This attitude was fine for a feudal, largely agrarian society; but city dwellers felt the need for a more active understanding of their surroundings, in order to solve the new problems posed by urban life. (The problem of drainage, for instance, was particularly pressing.)

The scientific approach of Aristotle appeared to fit these needs. The medieval world was stirring from its slumbers, and technological advances were appearing. (The advent of the open sewer, for example.) Christian theology now found itself confronted, for the first time in its history, with the problem posed by scientific explanations of the world's workings. Where purely mystical contemplation had once reigned supreme, reason now began to raise its ugly head. (Faced with the almost unendurable foulness of the world, one could meditate hard on transcendent reality—or go and sluice out the sewer.)

This change of attitude was accompanied by a transformation in other spheres. In the courts the revival of the methods of Roman law was leading to the proper investigation of crimes, rather than attempts to discover the "truth" by subjecting defendants to ordeals, such as the ducking stool. (If they confessed, they were guilty and hanged; if they drowned when they were innocent, their souls went to heaven.) For one of those rare moments of history, it looked as if an increased element of reason was about to enter human affairs. Europe was on the brink of a Renaissance. (The fact that it didn't take place is another story. Thomas Aquinas was to play his part in this too. By rendering Aristotle's ideas harmless to church teaching, he helped postpone the inevitable. And this was further postponed in the fourteenth century by the arrival of the Black Death, which left a trail of dead bodies, and exhumed a trail of dead ideas, throughout Europe.)

When Aquinas arrived in Paris with Albertus Magnus, he took up residence in the Latin Quarter, which received its name from the language spoken by the international community of students that thronged its narrow streets. Aquinas is known to have stayed on the Rue St. Jacques, then the quarter's main street, at the College of Jacobins (the French Dominicans). After taking his bachelor's degree, Aquinas, now thirty years old, received his license to teach. The tall, lumbering youth had undergone a transformation.

31

Beneath his staring oxlike eyes sprouted a dark bushy beard; meanwhile the upper part of his head had become completely bald. Aquinas's hagiographers speak of his austere life and frugal habits, yet most descriptions also mention his vast potbelly. The only way I can see round this protruding conundrum is that he probably ate rather a lot, but absentmindedly.

Despite Aquinas's unprepossessing appearance and retiring social manner, he quickly became a favorite with students, and his lectures began attracting large crowds. This was the man who had absorbed the latest available teachings of Aristotle and could render even his most abstruse ideas comprehensible to all.

But the ideas of Aristotle were not popular with conservative church authorities. By the time Aquinas arrived on the scene in Paris, Aristotle's teaching had already been condemned no less than four times for leading the faithful astray. (In 1231 Pope Gregory IX even appointed a commission to expurgate examples of reason from the works of Aristotle.) But Aquinas did his best to steer clear of controversy with the church. According to his interpretation of Aristotle, theology could now become a science. Based on self-evident principles and the truth revealed by God (in the Bible), a framework of knowledge could be built according to rational principles. (Four centuries later Spinoza was to construct his entire philosophy according to this blueprint.)

Still, there was one controversy which Aquinas could not avoid—that between the university authorities and the Dominicans. The university authorities were loathe to recognize the newly founded Dominicans and grant them the privilege of exemption from the civil law enjoyed by other members of the university. In the eyes of the authorities, the impoverished Dominicans, in their tatty black robes, were no better than licensed beggars and vagabonds. The Dominicans responded by refusing to recognize the authority of the university, yet insisted that legally they were entitled to the same freedoms as all other members of the university, that is, freedom from the jurisdiction of the civil authorities. The controversy between the Dominicans and the university authorities came to a head in 1257 when Thomas Aquinas was appointed professor of philosophy at Paris. Those who backed the university against the Dominicans refused to countenance this Dominican appointment, and appealed to the pope.

The Dominicans may have preached otherworldliness, but they were no slouches when it came to dealing with the problems of this world. Especially the very worldly world of church politics. Before embarking on their tussle with the University of Paris, the Dominicans had astutely taken precautions. Crucially, they had made sure they had influence at the Curia, the papal court—with the result that the pope eventually decided in their favor. Aquinas's appointment was confirmed. And as a result of this appointment, the Dominicans now acquired respectability at universities and courts throughout Europe.

Aquinas continued teaching and went on writing the magnum opus that he had begun after taking his degree. This was *Summa Contra Gentiles* (*A Summary of Arguments Against the*

34

Disbelievers), which contains much of his finest philosophical work as well as long passages which demonstrate to Catholics that the only true philosophy remains beyond human understanding. (This seemingly self-defeating philosophical position—claiming that philosophical truth is in fact incomprehensible—has a long tradition. Indeed, it even extends to modern philosophy, with Wittgenstein insisting that such truth is so unspeakably incomprehensible that we mustn't even talk about it.)

Summa Contra Gentiles is an encyclopedic work which incorporates the thinking of Aristotle into the theology of the Catholic church, in much the same way as St. Augustine had incorporated the thought of Plato into Christian doctrine eight centuries earlier. As we have seen, before Aquinas's vast and detailed analysis of Aristotle's ideas, and his relation of them to Christian ideas, Christian theology had been coming under increasing pressure from the rediscovery of Greek culture, with its emphasis on reason and science. Indeed, it's difficult to see how Christian theology of the period could have survived without Aquinas's help.

Summa Contra Gentiles is a philosophical work whose purpose is strictly unphilosophical. In it, Aquinas uses philosophical arguments to demonstrate the truth of Christian beliefs. His arguments are aimed at the thoughtful non-Christian. This species was generally held to be extinct in Europe during the period; and whenever such proved not to be the case, vigorous inquisitorial measures were taken to ensure that it *did* become the case. So who was Aquinas writing for? His imaginary reader is generally reckoned to be an intellectual Arab. After being subjected to hundreds of pages demonstrating the incontrovertible truth of the Christian religion, it is assumed that he has no alternative but to forswear Islam and embrace Christianity. How many intellectual Arabs subjected themselves to this grueling experience and reached the same conclusion is unknown.

Aquinas's purpose may be suspect, but his philosophizing is of a high caliber. His arguments follow simply and logically from step to step, echoing the manner adopted in Plato's dialogues and the works of Aristotle. He likes to begin with the commonplace particular and lead, step by step, to the most profound conclusions. Take for instance his notion of "wisdom." It is possible, he says, to achieve wisdom in some practical sphere, such as the making of money. Here the wisdom is the means employed for a particular purpose (getting rich). But all particular purposes are subsumed in the overall purpose of the world. This purpose is the ultimate truth, which is good. The highest form of wisdom thus leads us toward an understanding of this overall purpose: God's will.

Those who do not accept that the ultimate purpose of the world is good may feel there is a gap in this line of reasoning. But there is no denying the leading role of reason in such argument, which Aquinas derived from Aristotle. According to Aquinas, such informed reasoning will always lead us toward God. But it can only take us so far. We can use reason to prove such things as the existence of God and the immortality of the soul. But reason is incapable of proving the existence of such things as the Last Judgment and the Holy Ghost. The existence of these can only be understood by revelation, which comes from faith.

Aquinas is at great pains to differentiate between the realm of reason and that of faith. Truths that can be demonstrated by reason never contradict the truths of faith. Likewise the truths of faith, which are discovered by revelation, are always in accord with the truths discovered by reason. Fortunately, most of *Summa Contra Gentiles* is devoted to the latter, and only when these reasonable arguments reach their conclusion does Aquinas point out how they accord with the truths of faith.

Aquinas's classification of reason subtly clears the way for independent scientific investigation, using the methods of Aristotle. At the same time it stresses how the conclusions drawn from such investigations are bound to agree with the tenets of faith. It gives the appearance of an equal partnership between reason and faith—but this equality is an illusion. The church had long since made a meal of science. And in doing so it had swallowed Aristotle whole (or at least those bones of his philosophy that had survived the Dark Ages in western Europe). Aristotle's science was now a part of the faith. The world was made up of earth, air, fire, and water; the earth was the center of the universe; a heavy object dropped to the ground faster than a light object. Aristotle had written that such things were true, so they *were* true (even when anyone dropping a book and a pen at the same time could immediately see otherwise).

The main difficulty for Aquinas's argument arose when Aristotle's reason was applied to the very science he had produced. Here reason and faith *did* come into conflict. But for the time being this difficulty was brushed under the carpet, where it would remain for three centuries, until the advent of Copernicus and Galileo. (Copernicus essentially used mathematical reasoning to demonstrate that the planets circled the sun. Galileo's reliance on experimental method can be seen as an extension of reason into the practical sphere. Aristotle would certainly have recognized both these as developments of the logic that he had invented. Aristotle had never intended his science to be static. He rightly saw it as a continuing process of investigation. Only the *method* was meant to be a permanent feature.)

If the church had only distinguished Aristotle's method (reason, logic, categorization) from his findings, the conflict with science would never have arisen. Aristotle's scientific findings could then have been seen as a necessary limitation of his age, like his form of dress or his unavoidable pagan status. This is best illustrated by a conflict that *didn't* arise. Aristotle barely mentioned commercial practice, and thus the birth of merchant banking which took place around this period infringed no articles of faith (other than the Bible's edict on usury, which was cynically circumvented). Aristotle had made no pronouncements on double-entry bookkeeping or rates of interest on loans. As a result, the "science of money" was able to develop unhindered, to the immense profit of European civilization (and of course the bankers).

But back to *Summa Contra Gentiles*. Having

cleared the ground for reason, Aquinas now set about using it for a fundamental task—proving the existence of God. Nowadays we tend to regard this as one of the things reason *cannot* be used to prove. The existence of God is self-evident to us, a matter of faith. Or we consider the whole thing a fairy tale. No matter how compelling and reasonable the arguments, either for or against, these appear irrelevant. In other words, we now tend to consider that such things as the existence of God and the immortality of the soul fall into the realm of revelation. What is philosophically important is Aquinas's delineation of these two categories (reason, revelation), not his misapplication of them. As we have already seen, something remarkably similar to these categories still continues in modern philosophy, where Wittgenstein maintains: "Whereof one cannot speak, one must remain silent." Or, put another way: any ultimate truth, if there is such a thing, is so beyond proof that we cannot even talk about it.

It is useful to adopt a similar attitude when considering Aquinas's actual proofs of the existence of God. What is interesting is not so much the conclusions as the arguments themselves. In other words, the form of such arguments.

The literal-minded have every right to be suspicious at this point. Such an attitude can be highly dangerous. (The form of argument used by a racist or a flat-earther may be superior to that adopted by us cosmopolitan globalists, though this doesn't make the conclusion of their argument any less preposterous.) Proofs of God's existence may have passed out of fashion, but their form remains very much with us. Indeed, as we shall see, contemporary scientists now use one such form to explain the existence of the universe.

Curiously, Aquinas begins by rejecting what many consider to be the most compelling proof of God's existence, namely, the Ontological Argument—which had been formulated just over a century before Aquinas was born.

The man responsible for the Ontological Argument was St. Anselm, an Italian monk who became Archbishop of Canterbury during the reign of William Rufus. He quarreled with the king over some chalice covers, and was exiled; later, Henry I recalled him, but they too quarreled, and Anselm was exiled once more. He was obviously pretty good at arguments—but the Ontological Argument was far and away his finest. Put very simply, this starts with an assertion with which most people would agree (even if they don't believe in God). It states that the idea of God is the greatest possible idea of which we can conceive. According to Anselm, if this idea doesn't actually exist, there must be an even greater idea exactly like it which also includes the attribute of existence. Thus the greatest of all ideas must exist, otherwise an even greater idea would be possible, Q.E.D., God exists.

Aquinas rejected this argument on the grounds that we on earth can only gain a vague conception of the attributes of God; we can never know all of them perfectly. Thus we cannot *prove* whether these include existence or not.

Despite being rejected by Aquinas, the Ontological Argument was to have a long and fascinating intellectual pedigree. Four centuries later it was taken up by Descartes, and then adopted in variant forms by both Spinoza and Leibniz. In the following century Kant was to agree with Aquinas and reckoned he'd destroyed the Ontological Argument once and for all—but something very similar to it surfaces again in the philosophy of Hegel. Arguments for the existence of God may now be considered redundant, but they were to provide an element of continuity in philosophy long after it had freed itself from the straitjacket of theology (so skillfully tailored for it by Aquinas). And though the Ontological Argument may now have fallen from fashion in philosophy, it has recently made an astonishing comeback in the realm of science. Some cosmologists have begun using it to explain how the universe began. They argue as follows: Before the Big Bang nothing existed. All was nothingness, which was devoid of the attribute of existence. But this "all," in order to become truly All, *had* to take on existence. This necessity is dressed up in quasi-scientific terms, but its logic is recognizably medieval.

Yet this unexpected revival is not unique. No less a figure than Stephen Hawking also uses a very similar argument in his best-selling *A Brief History of Time*. In this he discusses whether we will ever be able to come up with a unified theory (one which will provide the ultimate explanation of how the universe works—that is, a theory of everything). At one point Hawking asks, "Is the unified theory so compelling that it brings about its own existence?" He appears to concur with the Ontological Argument by suggesting that it does.

As we have seen, Aquinas would have had no truck with such explanations of the Big Bang or a Theory of Everything. He had his own ideas on topics that professed to explain how the world began and how it worked. These were neatly encapsulated in the proof of God's existence that he sets out in *Summa Contra Gentiles*. It is essentially a rewording of Aristotle's Prime Mover Argument. Aquinas states that "everything which is moved is moved by another thing." This chain of cause and effect can be traced in a regressive series. But no such series can be infinite. Thus we eventually arrive at the prime mover, which is itself unmoved. In the words of Aquinas: "All understand that this is God." Although it's worth pointing out that Aristotle's original Prime Mover Argument, conceived in the fourth century B.C., could hardly have led to the Christian idea of God. It didn't even lead Aristotle to the precursor Judaic God who appears in the Old Testament. In fact it led him to the very dissimilar ancient Greek idea of deity. This involved several dozen *different* gods—whose licentious behavior was scarcely in accord with Christian morality. (Here Aristotle may well have been bowing to contemporary prejudice. On other occasions he appears to have regarded God as a kind of supreme intellect or spirit. Which goes to show that even if we do accept Aristotle's Prime Mover Argument, this can prove the existence of any kind of deity—from the god of mathematics to a little goat-legged flute player who ravages nymphs.)

Aquinas's Prime Mover Argument carries some weight in a mechanistic universe, even if its conclusion is less than compelling to the scientist. (Suppose the Big Bang were caused by some infinitely compressed particle; why should we understand this as God?) Also, the argument falls down in a mathematical universe, which *does* have infinite series. These were not unknown in Aquinas's time. He would have known of incommensurables, such as π, which are referred to in Euclid—whose recently translated work had done so much to kindle the medieval love of geometry.

Such arguments may seem unfair. How could Aquinas have taken into account the notion of the Big Bang, which was only conceived in the twentieth century? And wouldn't he have considered mathematical incommensurables irrelevant, arguing that mathematics was an abstract pursuit, not part of the particular world of cause and effect?

In other aspects Aquinas's philosophy is largely realistic. Like Aristotle, he was inclined to adopt an empirical approach: our knowledge derives basically from our experience. Aquinas's approach was famously described by the flamboyant early-twentieth-century Catholic writer G. K. Chesterton as "organized common sense." This is of course ludicrous—but appears less so if we view Aquinas in light of his time. In the thirteenth century many Aristotelian ideas had been accepted for so long that they were looked upon as common sense. It was "common sense" that the sun went around the earth, for instance. Other Aristotelian notions may appear less plausible, but it is still possible to understand how they seemed utterly convincing in their time.

For example, it was "common sense" that the world consisted ultimately of earth, air, fire, and water. This is of course rubbish, backed by neither experience nor experiment. It is pure conjecture. But it takes on much more force if, like Aristotle and the medievalists, you regarded the world from a *qualitative* point of view. Then the constituents of the world could easily be seen as a blend of such qualities. After all, our actual experience of the world through our senses *is* basically qualitative. Sweet, sour, hot, cold, bright. . . . Earth, air, fire, and water are merely deductions from these premises.

Such was the worldview that Aquinas accepted from Aristotle—the paradigm, or mindset, that was characteristic of medieval philosophy. Its limitations become apparent only when compared with the mind-set we have chosen to adopt. This is essentially *quantitative*. Instead of seeing in terms of qualities, we prefer to see in terms of measurement. (This is the main reason why medieval mathematics was regarded as fundamentally abstract, whereas ours describes everything from subatomic particles to the farthest reaches of the universe.)

The quantitative approach too had its origins in ancient Greece. Democritus said the world was made up of indivisible atoms; Archimedes applied mathematics to practical problems such as levers, pulleys, and hydrostatics. But this approach was disregarded by the Aristotelian tradition. Its readoption around the time of the Renaissance marked the beginnings of modern science. Yet it is worth reiterating that the quantitative is not the only approach. The medieval mind-set may appear quaint to our world of quantum physics and black holes, but our approach is not without its flaws. And some of these were not apparent in the medieval paradigm. The formulas of physics can explain the occurrence of the rainbow and can even show what colors it will exhibit. But they cannot account for its quality—the sheer beauty that is its most immediate property. Modern scientists are not unaware of this failing. No less a figure than the great quantum physicist Richard Feynman once said: "The test of science is its ability to predict. Had you never visited the earth, could you predict the thunderstorms, the volcanoes, the ocean waves, the auroras, and the colorful sunset? . . . The next great era of awakening of human intellect may well produce a method of understanding the qualitative content of equations. . . . Today we cannot see whether 'a quantum mechanical' equation contains frogs, musical composers, or morality—or whether it does not." So the "next great era of human knowledge" could well involve taking on board the medieval approach!

Aquinas continued to work on *Summa Contra Gentiles* for several years, but before he could complete his great work he was appointed to the curia as an adviser. In 1259 he returned to Italy to take up his post at Anagni, in the hills thirty miles south of Rome, where Pope Alexander IV had set up his court in his hometown. (In those days the pope preferred to rule from a safe haven. The streets of Rome were infested with pickpockets, thieves, and muggers who preyed on innocent tourists and passersby, but unlike today they also preyed on the popes.)

Pope Alexander IV, whose real name was Rinaldo, came from a well-known papal family. (His uncle had been Pope Gregory IX.) Alexander IV is best remembered for his enthusiastic encouragement of the Inquisition in France, and his persistently unsuccessful attempts to promote a crusade against the Mongols. (For some reason, no one fancied setting out across hundreds of miles of barren steppe to stir up a hornets' nest, and the hordes of Genghis Khan's successor were left in peace.) Unfortunately Alexander was so busy with all this that he forgot to appoint any cardinals. This meant that there were only eight cardinals left when he died in 1261, two years after Aquinas's arrival. These aged cardinals were duly summoned for the conclave to elect a new pope, but couldn't agree which of them should get the job. So in the end they gave it to the patriarch of Jerusalem, who happened to be in town on a visit from the Holy Land. This was a Frenchman called Pantaleon, who wisely decided to take on the name of Urban IV. So Aquinas now found himself serving under a new pope, who began his reign in Orvieto but later moved to Perugia because he was afraid of being poisoned.

During Aquinas's period with the curia he completed *Summa Contra Gentiles*, wrote commentaries on the Gospels, composed some fine hymns which demonstrate his skill as a poet, and completed commentaries on the works of Aristotle, sermons, texts, and a treatise pointing out the errors in Greek philosophy. The sheer quantity of Aquinas's works is as voluminous as that of any other major philosopher before or since, but his use of secretaries means that his style is often rather pedestrian. He is said to have been able to dictate to four secretaries at a time— though in the days of quill pens, elaborate italic script, and clerical secretaries more attuned to a medieval pace in the office, this may not have been quite the quick-witted intellectual juggling feat it initially appears.

Aquinas also spent a large amount of his time at the curia drawing up preparations for the union of the Catholic Church of Rome with the Byzantine Church of Constantinople. This was a project cherished by many popes. Intricate negotiations took place, compromises were mooted, detailed documents were drawn up, and on occasion meetings even took place between the two parties—but all to little avail. The Catholics were far too byzantine in their approach, and the Byzantines remained incorrigibly byzantine.

Aquinas was not the only great philosopher to play a leading role in attempting to unite Christendom. In the seventeenth century the German philosopher Leibniz was instrumental in an equally doomed move to unite the Roman Catholic and Protestant churches. (By then Byzantium had long since been overrun by the Turks.) Among the great philosophers, Aquinas was unusual in playing a major role in the practical affairs of his day, and doubly unusual in the fact that his peers took this role seriously. Leibniz's plans were a highly sophisticated work of genius, far too subtle to be taken seriously.

Aquinas adopted the Aristotelian attitude to politics—that is to say, a pragmatic approach which at least had a chance of working. When Aristotle had drawn up a new constitution for any city state, his first criterion had been whether it could be put into practice in that city state. Only then would he attempt to incorporate all the best features from the constitutions of other city states. Aquinas did on several occasions draw up a series of skillful compromises between the practices of the Western and Eastern churches, but negotiations were hamstrung by the interested parties' profound antipathy to the first principle of politics, as understood by both Aristotle and Aquinas (and precious few political philosophers before or since). All attempts by Aquinas to smuggle this principle into the negotiations were confounded.

Aquinas's political practice was undeniably practical, but his political theory was just as undeniably theoretical. For Aquinas, the state was the perfect society. But the state could not be too oppressive because the rightful moral aim of man in this life is human happiness. This may be vague, but at least it is anchored in Aristotelian common sense—and it is even fairly serviceable as a general principle. Unfortunately Aquinas was far too much of an intellectual to let such vagueness stand. He now introduced an element of Aristotelian thought whose flimsy attachment to common sense in ancient Greece had worn somewhat threadbare over the centuries. One of the tenets of Aristotelian metaphysics was that the part is adjusted to the whole in the same way as the imperfect is adjusted to the perfect. So, as the individual is part of a perfect society, the law must be concerned with human happiness (because in a perfect society we should all be happy). This argument bears thinking through in some detail, as its steps and implications are admirably subtle. But when all is said and done, it introduces no new element of clarity to the original vagueness which it set out to dispel.

Fortunately Aquinas's skills as a political theorist were never misapplied to reality. His practical skills as a political operator, however, were much appreciated and frequently in demand. Late in 1268 Aquinas was hurriedly dispatched on an important mission to Paris. Once again the university was in a turmoil of controversy. The dispute between the Dominicans and the university authorities had reopened. At the same time recent translations of Averroës's commentaries on Aristotle were leading to dangerous radicalism. Aquinas had the difficult task of defending the Dominicans while defending his belief in Aristotle from attacks on all sides. The traditionalists considered that recent developments were compromising orthodox beliefs and placing the entire Christian interpretation of Aristotle in jeopardy. The Averroists (as the radicals were now called) had fastened once more on the old division between reason and faith. According to them, these represented two entirely different forms of knowledge, namely, religious knowledge on the one hand, and scientific, rational knowledge on the other. In their view, the knowledge of faith and the knowledge of reason were utterly independent—and could even contradict each other. This revolutionary split (which still runs beneath the surface of our thinking today) was correctly seen as a direct threat to the intellectual dictatorship of the church.

Aquinas continued his defense of theology as a "science of reason," based on revealed religious principles. But this sanctioning of the autonomy of reason, even within the boundaries of faith, led many traditionalists to condemn him along with the Averroists.

Apart from all this, Aquinas also had his work cut out trying to defend the Dominicans. Much of the underlying cause of these struggles was political rather than purely intellectual, but fortunately Aquinas had some powerful allies. Not least of these was Louis IX, king of France.

Louis IX was in many ways the exemplar of a medieval monarch. A muddled, well-meaning man, he ruled France for more than forty years. He enjoyed intellectual company: the founder of the Sorbonne was a close friend of his, and bright clerics such as Aquinas were regular guests at his dinner table. Louis achieved renown throughout Europe for his unprecedented diplomatic behavior. He actually kept his word, and even conformed to treaties he had signed—practices as rare in the thirteenth century as they are in the twentieth. Louis was also an avid builder of churches, his most famous being Saint-Chapelle in Paris, which he built to accommodate an extremely rare relic given to him by the Emperor Baldwin of Byzantium (Christ's Crown of Thorns, of which there were only three genuine originals at the time).

But Louis is perhaps best remembered for his crusades. In 1248 he set out on the Sixth Crusade. All went well until 1250 when Louis was defeated and captured at Al Mansura in Egypt. He was held in Syria for four years while the usual negotiations for the release of Middle Eastern hostages got under way. Louis's release was finally agreed in exchange for a colossal sum of money (a king's ransom, no less) and the surrender of all the territory he had gained on the crusade.

After this, many thought that Louis's crusading days were over—but within a few years he was busily planning another one. He finally set out for the Holy Land once more in 1270. Unfortunately he caught a fever not long after disembarking from France, and had to be put ashore at Tunis, where he died. Twenty-seven years later he was canonized, and is now famous throughout Missouri and for his blues.

King Louis had great respect for Thomas Aquinas. One of the few credible anecdotes about Aquinas relates how he went to a ceremonial banquet given by the king. As the king was talking he was suddenly interrupted by one of his guests bringing his fist down with a crash onto the table. The hall fell silent, and all turned to stare at the large, potbellied cleric responsible—who appeared to be unaware of the disturbance he had caused. Deep in thought, Aquinas muttered to himself: "I have it!"

The king leaned down the table, unused to being interrupted in such a fashion, and demanded an explanation. Aquinas came to himself and looked about him. "I am sorry, your majesty," he apologized. "But I have just realized how to refute Manichaeism."

Louis was so impressed by the blundering

otherworldly cleric that instead of reprimanding him, he ordered Aquinas to continue with his meditations—and dispatched a secretary to take down his refutation of Manichaeism. This quasi-Christian heresy, dating from the third century, believed that the world was a product of the conflict between Good and Evil, or light and darkness. The human soul consisted of light, entrapped by darkness from which it must seek to free itself. The profound simplicity and coherence of this core dualistic doctrine, which echoed pre-Christian Mediterranean cults, made Manichaeism prevalent throughout the Mediterranean world, from early Christian times until well into the medieval era. (In the fourth century St. Augustine was a Manichaean, before his conversion.)

Aquinas refuted Manichaeism by denying its dualism. Evil does not exist as a positive entity; it is merely a lack of properly informed good. Even when committing the most evil acts, we always have good in mind (even if only our own). The psychology of this would seem irrefutable. The murderer sees the death of his victim as good; even the unwilling torturer conforms because he considers it better to do so. The fact that our view of good is mistaken is what makes it evil. Despite being intellectually routed by Aquinas, and actually routed by less intellectually minded opponents (the Albigensian Massacre, and so forth), Manichaeism obstinately persisted until well into the fifteenth century, and possibly beyond. Indeed, recently uncovered historical evidence suggests that it may even have been covertly imported to the New World by early settlers.

But Aquinas had more to do in Paris than refute heresies over dinner. He had been sent on a mission. As part of his campaign to defend the Dominicans and resist the inroads on Aristotelianism by the firebrand Averroists, Augustine wrote a treatise. This he called *De Pestifera Doctrina Retrahentium Homines a Religionis Ingressa* (which could be loosely translated: All about the pestilential doctrine put forward by retrogrades who wish to drag us all back into the Dark Ages). Perhaps as a result of its catchy title, this treatise soon became a best-seller throughout the Latin Quarter, and Aquinas carried the day.

In 1272 Aquinas returned to Italy and took up a teaching post at his alma mater in Naples. Here he continued to work on his second magnum opus, *Summa Theologica*, an attempt to bring together all the separate elements of his thought into a comprehensive philosophical system. This system was intended to include all the moral, intellectual, and theological thought of the Catholic church. Although this work remained incomplete at Aquinas's death, it is still considered the finest and most complete exposition of the medieval mind—sadly, a somewhat hollow achievement in modern eyes. Aquinas's masterpiece attracts virtually no interest today, except among Catholics, who have to study it because it contains the truth about philosophy.

The tone is set when Aquinas gives no less than five proofs for the existence of God. (Modern readers may wonder why, if one is not enough, four more will do the trick any better.) Other topics which have ensured Aquinas's masterpiece the slimmest chance of entering the best-

seller lists include discussions of the following:
"what the world will be like after judgment,"
"whether weakness, ignorance, malice, and lust
are the result of sin," and "whether the move-
ment of the heavenly bodies will cease after
Judgment Day." You may find it difficult to believe that even during the medieval era people
were able to summon great enthusiasm for such
topics, accompanied as they were by Aquinas's
copious dissertations on their pros and cons,
together with ample quotations from "the
philosopher" (Aristotle) and other long-dead authorities. But you would be wrong. During this
period vast numbers of monasteries were scattered throughout the length and breadth of Europe, many in extremely remote locations.
Within the confines of these so-called ab-
stemious and celibate institutions, the lower or-
ders did most of the turnip picking and beer
tasting—leaving the intellectuals to combat the
disease that reached epidemic proportions
throughout monastic Europe, namely *accidie*,
often known as "the sickness of monks," better
known to us as stupefying apathy or sloth.

Under such circumstances, Aquinas's long and earnest discussions on "whether the body is commanded by the soul in irrational animals," "the bodily condition and identity of those who rise again after death," and "whether we should love our body out of charity" must indeed have proved riveting topics.

Fortunately Aquinas was interested in writing something more than Christianity's answer to the Talmud. Amidst all the rabbinical nitpicking there are passages which reveal a mind in a class of its own, whose thought is way ahead of its time. Take for instance Aquinas's discussion of whether pain or sorrow is assuaged by every pleasure. He begins by quoting "the philosopher": "Sorrow is driven out by pleasure, either by a contrary pleasure or by any other, as long as it is intense." Aquinas then argues: "Pleasure is a kind of repose of the appetite in a suitable good, while sorrow arises from something unsuited to the appetite." He concludes, in a passage whose slightly outdated approach should not be allowed to obscure its insight: "A person can find himself filled with sadness when he takes part in some pleasant activity which he used to share with a friend who is now absent or dead. Under such circumstances there are two causes within him, which produce contradictory effects. The thought of his friend's absence causes sorrow to well up in him. On the other hand, his life in the immediate present, participating in pleasant activity, is a cause of pleasure. Each of these causes in some way modifies the other. But our perception of the present is stronger than our memory of the past. Also our love of self is more persistent than our love for another. Thus, in the end, our pleasure drives out our sorrow."

Here Aquinas reveals psychological acumen while miraculously remaining within an orthodox religious standpoint which also agrees with his Aristotelian philosophy. Writing insightful psychology is difficult enough, especially in the language of a pre-psychological era. Writing psychology, which is at the same time also theology *and* philosophy, is a major intellectual juggling trick.

This brings us to Aquinas's moral philosophy. Once again he adopts the commonsense Aristotelian approach. Aristotle, and Aquinas, saw human happiness as the goal of all in this life. Sailing through life with this attitude may carry one perilously close to the reefs of unorthodoxy and even heresy, though Aquinas had sufficient skill and psychological acumen to disguise this awkward fact. The aim of moral philosophy was to delineate how this happiness could be achieved in a moral fashion—for the individual, the family, and society. Such happiness, said Aquinas, was achieved by way of the "natural law," which was discovered by reason. This natural law could also be rejected, thus making immoral behavior irrational and unnatural. As we have already seen, unreasonable behavior is usually adopted for selfish reasons, when we have a mistaken, shortsighted idea of happiness (for example, murder, greed, or sloth).

Aquinas sets out four cardinal virtues which assist us in achieving moral goodness. These are prudence, justice, fortitude, and temperance. Of these, the major virtue is prudence. To modern eyes this may appear a somewhat vague, prissy concept: the element of discrete discernment in action. The actual Latin word Aquinas uses is *prudentia*. This is a stronger notion, with connotations of wisdom, foresight, and skill (both social and intellectual). Yet it remains somewhat vague as a guideline. Aquinas appears to mean that we should cultivate in ourselves a suitable perception which enables us to come out on the side of the morally good. This may seem to us little more than "pick the winner" (ethically speaking, of course). But we live in uncertain times, when the ethical field has many runners. In Aquinas's day this was a one-horse race: the church was the invariable winner. The vagueness in his concept of prudence simply allowed for slight shifts in the church's position on moral matters.

For more than a year Aquinas continued lecturing at the University of Naples, working on his *Summa Theologica* and overworking on his usual prolific production of treatises, commentaries, sermons, works of exegesis, and the like. Then, in the autumn of 1273, while working late one night in his cell, he had a mystical experience. In the midst of this he saw a vision of the Truth and the joy of life everlasting. Afterward he gave up writing and became more solitary, explaining that all his intellectual arguments now seemed like "mere chaff in the wind." As winter drew on he became ill. Although he was only fifty, years of overwork and absentminded frugal living had taken their toll on even his robust frame. Aquinas now had only a few months to live.

In the New Year a summons arrived from Pope Gregory X, demanding Aquinas's presence at the Second Council of Lyons. This had been called in yet another attempt to heal the doctrinal rift between the Roman and the Byzantine churches. Aquinas was needed to explain the finer points of how their irreconcilable differences could still theoretically be overcome.

Heedless of his illness, Aquinas set off on the six-hundred-mile journey, which he was never to complete. By now he was barely aware of his surroundings. But as he journeyed north on the road from Naples, he found himself dimly recognizing the landscape around Aquino. On the hill

across the valley, above the village of Roccasecca, he made out the familiar silhouette of
the castle where he was born in 1225.

Afterword

The philosophy of St. Thomas Aquinas, later known as Thomism, was quickly adopted wholesale by the church. His works were consulted on doctrinal problems, and his philosophy became the ultimate intellectual authority. (The pope, of course, remained the ultimate actual authority, but his decrees usually had little intellectual content.)

This had a stifling effect on philosophical thought, which was reduced to mere quibblings about what Aristotle and Aquinas had actually meant. Commentary and exegesis were the order of the day, and original philosophy remained stone dead. (It's arguable that this had in fact

71

been the case since the death of St. Augustine, almost eight hundred years *before* Aquinas arrived on the scene.)

This outlook continued after the death of Aquinas and for the two remaining centuries of the medieval era. Astonishingly, it then persisted during the Renaissance, when the mind-set of European civilization changed beyond recognition. The earth, and the Roman Catholic church, were dislodged from the center of the universe. Science and humanism held sway, inspiring an intellectual self-confidence that enabled Europeans to circumnavigate the globe and redraw the map of the heavens. Yet philosophy remained unaffected, with Thomism continuing to be taught in the universities, and the world of speculation caught in a two-thousand-year-old Aristotelian time warp.

Not until the seventeenth century did the first cracks begin to appear in this vast Gothic structure, upon which more concerted labor and gargoylean ingenuity had been lavished than on any work of man before or since. Then, in 1637, Descartes published his *Discourse on Method*. In this he questioned all the previously accepted certainties of the world, arriving at one bedrock notion upon which all thought could be based. This was his famous dictum "Cogito ergo sum" ("I think, therefore I am"). Modern philosophy had begun, and the cobwebs of Aristotle and Thomism were swept away forever.

From Aquinas's Writings

Aquinas's famous "prime mover" proof of the existence of God:

Anything that is in nature must be moved by something else. Likewise this something else, in so far as it too is in motion, must also be moved by something else. Similarly that too must be moved by yet another thing. But this chain of events cannot recede forever, for if it did there could be no first mover and thus no other mover. For second movers cannot move unless they are moved by a first mover, in the same way that a stick does not move anything unless it is moved by a hand. In this way we must reach a prime mover which is not itself moved by anything. And all understand that this is God.

—*Summa Theologica*

The basis of Aquinas's refutation of the Onto-logical Argument:

We can never know what God is, only what He is not. Therefore we must reflect upon the ways in which He is not, rather than the ways in which He is.

—*Summa Theologica*

An example of where Aquinas's reliance on Aristotle is so admirable in principle but less practical in application:

As Aristotle shows, we should proceed as follows when studying a particular class of things. First we should attempt to discover the qualities which all members of this class hold in common. Only then should we study the special qualities of the differing individuals within it. . . . There is a class of things which includes all living creatures. So the best way to study the members of this class is first to discover what qualities they have in common, and only later what special qualities are possessed by different members.

There is one thing common to every living thing. This is the soul—for all living creatures possess a soul. Therefore to discover knowledge about living creatures, the best way to proceed is first to study the soul, which is present in each one of them.

—Commentary on Aristotle's *De Anima*
(*Concerning the Soul*)

But this approach is not quite so laughably out-moded as it might appear. The quality *that set living things apart was the soul. Subsequent quantitative investigations have been unable to locate this elusive entity. But there remains no doubt that this concept reflected some element of our experience. Science thus retreated to the more empirically safe notion of "consciousness."*

Yet this too has now come under increasing fire. What precisely is consciousness? The quantitative approach finds extreme difficulty with such problems, which nonetheless remain fundamental to our notion of our existence. Perhaps such problems will be resolved only when we reincorporate the qualitative approach adopted by Aristotle, Aquinas, and medieval philosophy.

Dante's Divine Comedy *encapsulates the entire range of the medieval world and its thought. It provides us with an example of the relative esteem in which St. Thomas Aquinas and Aristotle were held. The ancient Greek philosopher is referred to as* il maestro di color che sanno *(the master of those who know). Later, Aquinas is referred to as* fiamma benedetta *(the flame of holy wisdom). Aristotle was the wisest of men, but only the word of Aquinas was regarded as having divine inspiration.*

The purpose of each thing is that which is intended by the creator or mover of that thing.

Now the prime mover or creator of the universe is spirit or mind. [Here Aquinas coopts an Aristotelian notion of God as mind or intellect.] For this reason the final end or purpose of the universe must be the good of the intellect. And this is truth. Thus truth must be the final purpose of the universe, and the pondering of truth must be the chief occupation of wisdom.

—*Summa Contra Gentiles:*
The Activity of the Wise

Chronology of Significant Philosophical Dates

6th C B.C.	The beginning of Western philosophy with Thales of Miletus.
End of 6th C B.C.	Death of Pythagoras.
399 B.C.	Socrates sentenced to death in Athens.
c 387 B.C.	Plato founds the Academy in Athens, the first university.
335 B.C.	Aristotle founds the Lyceum in Athens, a rival school to the Academy.

324 A.D.	Emperor Constantine moves capital of Roman Empire to Byzantium.
400 A.D.	St. Augustine writes his *Confessions*. Philosophy absorbed into Christian theology.
410 A.D.	Sack of Rome by Visigoths heralds opening of Dark Ages.
529 A.D.	Closure of Academy in Athens by Emperor Justinian marks end of Hellenic thought.
Mid-13th C	Thomas Aquinas writes his commentaries on Aristotle. Era of Scholasticism.
1453	Fall of Byzantium to Turks, end of Byzantine Empire.
1492	Columbus reaches America. Renaissance in Florence and revival of interest in Greek learning.
1543	Copernicus publishes *On the Revolution of the Celestial Orbs*, proving mathematically that the earth revolves around the sun.

1633	Galileo forced by church to recant heliocentric theory of the universe.
1641	Descartes publishes his *Meditations*, the start of modern philosophy.
1677	Death of Spinoza allows publication of his *Ethics*.
1687	Newton publishes *Principia*, introducing concept of gravity.
1689	Locke publishes *Essay Concerning Human Understanding*. Start of empiricism.
1710	Berkeley publishes *Principles of Human Knowledge*, advancing empiricism to new extremes.
1716	Death of Leibniz.
1739–1740	Hume publishes *Treatise of Human Nature*, taking empiricism to its logical limits.
1781	Kant, awakened from his "dogmatic slumbers" by Hume, publishes *Critique of Pure Reason*.

Great era of German metaphysics begins.

1807   Hegel publishes *The Phenomenology of Mind*, high point of German metaphysics.

1818   Schopenhauer publishes *The World as Will and Representation*, introducing Indian philosophy into German metaphysics.

1889   Nietzsche, having declared "God is dead," succumbs to madness in Turin.

1921   Wittgenstein publishes *Tractatus Logico-Philosophicus*, claiming the "final solution" to the problems of philosophy.

1920s   Vienna Circle propounds Logical Positivism.

1927   Heidegger publishes *Being and Time*, heralding split between analytical and Continental philosophy.

1943   Sartre publishes *Being and Nothingness*, advancing

Heidegger's thought and instigating existentialism.

1953   Posthumous publication of Wittgenstein's *Philosophical Investigations*. High era of linguistic analysis.

Chronology of Aquinas's Life

1225	Birth of Thomas d'Aquino at Roccasecca in southern Italy.
1239	Aquinas begins studies at University of Naples.
1244	Aquinas enters Dominican order of mendicant friars. Later abducted by his brothers on the road to Rome.
1244–1245	Aquinas imprisoned by mother at Roccasecca castle.
1245	Aquinas escapes and journeys to Paris on foot.

1248–1252	Aquinas studies with Albertus Magnus in Cologne.
1251	Aquinas ordained in Cologne.
1252–1259	Aquinas teaching in Paris and writing *Summa Contra Gentiles*.
1259	Aquinas appointed adviser to curia of Pope Alexander IV; leaves Paris for Italy.
1266	Aquinas begins *Summa Theologica*.
1268	Aquinas dispatched to Paris to deal with continuing conflict between university and Dominicans, and radicalism of Averroists.
1272	Aquinas returns to Italy.
1273	Aquinas has mystical experience and ceases writing.
1274	Aquinas summoned by Pope Gregory X to attend Second Council of Lyons. Falls ill and dies on journey north.

1323   Aquinas canonized by Pope John
               XXII.

1879   Pope Leo XIII declares the works
               of St. Thomas Aquinas to be the
               only true philosophy.

Recommended Reading

Thomas Aquinas, *Treatise on Happiness* (University of Notre Dame Press, 1983)

Thomas Aquinas, *Summa Theologica* (in Great Books of the Western World, volumes 19 and 20, published by Encyclopedia Britannica)

Frederick Copleston, *A History of Philosophy, Volume II: Medieval Philosophy, Augustine to Scotus* (Paulist Press, 1994)

Bertrand Russell, *A History of Western Philosophy* (Simon and Schuster, 1967)

James Weisheipl, *Friar Thomas D'Aquino* (Catholic University Press, 1983)

Index

A NOTE ON THE AUTHOR

Paul Strathern has lectured in philosophy and mathematics and now lives and writes in London. A Somerset Maugham prize winner, he is also the author of books on history and travel as well as five novels. His articles have appeared in a great many publications, including the *Observer* (London) and the *Irish Times*. His own degree in philosophy was earned at Trinity College, Dublin.